The Soul Surrender

30 Days to Let Go and Align Yourself with God's Will

Copyright @ 2021 by **Melissa Brown** All rights reserved Published by beyondthebookmedia.com All rights reserved. No part of this publication may be reproduced, distributed, or transmitted in any form or by any means, including photocopying, recording, or other electronic or mechanical methods, without the prior written permission of the publisher, except in the case of brief quotations embodied in critical reviews and certain other noncommercial uses permitted by copyright law. For permission requests, write to the publisher, addressed "Attention: Permissions Coordinator," at the address below. Limit of Liability/Disclaimer of Warranty: While the publisher and author have used their best efforts in preparing this book, they make no representations of warranties with respect to the accuracy or completeness of the contents of this book and specifically disclaim any implied warranties or merchantability or fitness for a particular purpose. No warranty may be created or extended by sales representatives or written sales materials. The advice and strategies contained herein may not be suitable for your situation. You should consult with a professional where appropriate. Neither the publisher nor author shall be liable for damages arising here from. Beyond The Book Media, LLC Alpharetta. GA www. beyondthebookmedia.com The publisher is not responsible for websites that are not owned by the publisher. **ISBN** –978-1-953788-45-0 **(Printed)**

The Soul Surrender

30 Days to Let Go and Align Yourself with God's Will

Melissa Brown

I dedicate this book to the beautiful ladies in the Soul Love Tribe who trusted me to go on a surrender journey in March 2020 before the whole world was met with circumstances that brought all of us to our knees. Thank you, ladies, for trusting me with your heart and being willing to let go simply because God said so. For sharing the message, and your continuous support for me, I am forever grateful.

Table of contents

Introduction	11
How to Use This Book	13
Surrender Your Questions	17
Surrender Your Busyness	21
Surrender What Used to Be	25
Surrender Your Timeline	27
Surrender All Soul Agreements	31
Surrender Your Need to Know The Way	35
Surrender Your Anger	39
Surrender the Fight	43
Surrender your Brokenness	47
Surrender your Need to Fix It	51
Surrender your Understanding	55
Surrender the Spirit of Lack	59
Surrender your Expectations	63
Surrender the Fantasy	67
Surrender your Goals	71

Surrender the Weight	75
Surrender Your Need to Be Liked	79
I Surrender Those Who Have Wounded Me	83
I Surrender My Mother & Father	87
I Surrender My Beliefs	91
I Surrender My Imperfections	95
I Surrender to Love	99
I Surrender to Peace	103
I Surrender to an Abundant Life	107
I Surrender to the Flow	111
I Surrender to My Growth	115
I Surrender My Resistance to Receive Support	119
I Surrender to My Greatness	123
I Surrender to Making Space in My Life	127
Surrender to Your Own Becoming	131
Next Steps	135

Introduction

What does it really mean to surrender? According to Webster, it is the act of relinquishing control over territory. It is to cease resistance to one's opponent and submit to that authority. Surrender can happen voluntarily or by force, but I hope you cease fighting and wrestling by choice. And this book is designed to help you do just that. The soul surrender is all about letting go. It's about letting go of your will so that God's will can be done in your life.

There is so much warring and fighting going on, but most of the fighting happens within ourselves if we are honest. It is a daily battle to decide how you are going to respond to life and who you are going to be. Everyone wants to be productive and successful, but there is a way that is far greater than the ways of man, human wisdom, and intellect.

After all, we have experienced in the past few years, I am clear that we desperately need God. But God isn't just interested in being your rescue when you are in trouble. God wants you. God wants all of you. In other words, He wants to sit on the throne of your heart and lead you in everything you do and say.

This modern-day culture emphasizes personal choice, preferences, and the free will to do whatever you want to do with your life. But if you are going to be a vessel that God can use, you must voluntarily give up your will for His way.

This is true in every aspect of life. God wants to lead you in your relationships, career, finances, health, and the core of who you are. You can't say God lives within you while you run off and go live somewhere else. In this season, you must abide. This has to be your conscious choice. This is the mountain you must willingly decide to climb.

Understand this, the level of your success will be determined by the level of your surrender. In this season, where extraordinary things are happening that defy the natural order and the usual seasonal patterns, the only place for you to be is in the will of God. And that means there will be times that you go right while everyone around you is going left. You will be listening to the voice within you telling you which way to go while others are reading every success book and mapping the stars. You are different. This means you move differently, and if you are bold enough to do that, you will get results that astonish the masses and surprise even you.

The battle you must fight is not just "out there" in the world but also within you. Wrestling with the old you is not to be underestimated. You would be surprised at how hard we are willing to fight for familiar limitations. So while your spirit will be desiring greater glory, your flesh will desperately want to keep things the way they were.

When you surrender, you literally lay down your weapons, which means you will be vulnerable. But you can't be a chosen vessel without it. Vulnerability is the oil that makes you authentic and effective. It is a constant reminder of your humanity and God's divinity.

Over the next 30 days, you will remove the layers that you didn't even know had developed in and around your heart. Pride wears a thick coat and has a way of blocking out all the elements that allow you to feel. And on this journey, feeling what you have been avoiding is critical. But I promise that God will meet you in the center of your heart and do what your avoidance and self-medicating could not do. Together, we will journey to the root of your need to control, which is always fear; and you will find the courage to look fear in the face and see it for what it is, an illusion. So much in this life has been built on what was never real. It is time for you to know the truth. Time for you to know who you are at a deep level. It's time you found out that you can't mess up God's plan for your life no matter how hard you try. So you can relax, let go of your impossible need for perfection and grow in God's grace.

How to Use This Book

Each day you will read the set devotional centered around letting go of one thing and embracing another. Every devotion has a scripture reference and/or a quote to help you to center your thoughts. If you read your devotional in the morning, the scripture and the affirmation become the perfect mantra to keep you grounded throughout the day.

In addition, there is a daily activity that may be reflective or more experiential in nature. These activities are critical in allowing God's healing to go beyond the surface of your life and free you from your roots. The activities can be anything from journal writing, taking a walk outside, writing a letter, or sitting quietly with your thoughts. Every activity has been intentionally selected for the specific surrender that God requires of you. I don't want you to merely have the appearance of liberation; I actually want to know that you are living free even after the next 30 days. So make a commitment to yourself and the work.

Expect deeply buried emotions to come up. You can't go digging around in your emotional closet without old stuff falling out. In addition to prayer and spiritual support, this may be the perfect opportunity to work with a counselor or other licensed professional who has been trained and specializes in your area of emotional need.

No matter what, decide that you won't give up. Surrender is the new strategy for success and the road less traveled by the world. But you are not of this world; you merely live here. In fact, you were strategically placed here for such a time as this. So don't miss your moment trying to prove something to other people or even to yourself.

You've exhausted yourself trying to do things your way. This is your divine invitation to try a more excellent way.

Day 1

Soul Surrender

Surrender Your Questions

Call to me and I will answer you and tell you great and unsearchable things you do not know.
Jeremiah 33:3 (NIV)

Whatever your question, love is always the answer. On this first day of the soul surrender, I invite you to give up living in the question and your constant need to know, what, when, why, and the how. To surrender means that you are willing to trust God's outcome. You are willing to let go of the process while also stepping into it.

At times, our questions are nothing more than another layer to protect us from the core of ourselves. Questions keep us believing we don't know what to think or do when the truth is always within us. Questions keep you from hearing your own voice because they keep you thinking the answer is outside of you.

But on this first day of this sacred journey, I invite you to give up your need to know; and become like a child who has absolute trust in her mother. Babies trust they will be fed, although they don't know where the food will come from. They trust they will have everything they need.

So when did you learn that life could no longer be trusted? When did you decide you must have the answer? Today begins your journey back to love and away from fear. Back to that place where you trusted the God within you. Back to when you saw the question as a spiritual quest, not for the answer, but for a deeper part of yourself.

Today's Affirmation:
I Am on a Journey to a Deeper Part of Myself

Today's Action:

What do you surrender your need to know? Using the journal prompt, "I surrender my need to know..." let your brain release the many questions that swirl around in your head that all too often distract your attention from the moment. Release your need to know how something from the past may have worked out if you had moved to a different city, if you had married, or stayed single. Make this your morning prayer, so you can begin to free yourself from the "what ifs" and live in this present moment.

Day 2

Soul Surrender

Surrender Your Busyness

"Be still and know that I am God. I will be exalted among the nations and in the earth."
Psalm 46:10 (NIV)

Why is it so hard to be still? What exactly are we so busy doing? Take a look at your life and really examine what you are doing and why you are doing it? The primary reason that relationships fail is because of communication. If we can't talk, if you don't have time to listen, then it is likely that there will be problems. Just think about the couples who can't even go to dinner without being distracted by their phones. The person we say we love is right there, but our attention is elsewhere. And over time, it is easy to conclude that the other person just doesn't care enough to make time for you.

But what if you are "that other person"? What if you are the one who is so busy that you have been missing all the signs? What if your agenda has taken precedence over just being present? You can't hear another person's heart if you are preoccupied with other things. And what if who you have been missing is God? The scripture says, "Be still and know...," to know something means you have had an experience, and you can't have an experience if you are everywhere but here.

So today, sit down. Not just physically, but in your spirit. Surrender your need to be everywhere and in everything. Today, just listen. God is always speaking, but our ears are not always primed to hear. God speaks through the babies. God speaks through His word and those we love. God can even speak in the blowing of the wind. But you must decide that you are available to listen. Welcome to The Soul School, boys and girls. Take a seat, be quiet and listen.

Today's Affirmation:
"I will be still until God speaks."

Today's Action:

Make a point to slow down today. Be present in all that you do. Slow your brain down and resist the temptation to be thinking about "what's next" tomorrow or what you need to do for next year. Be here now. And let that be enough.

Day 3

Soul Surrender

Surrender What Used to Be

"Is this not what we told you in Egypt, when we said, 'Leave us alone!' and 'Let us serve the Egyptians!'? Indeed, it would have been better for us to serve the Egyptians than to die in the desert!"

Exodus 14:12 (NIV)

Whenever we can't predict or expect a better future, we begin to long for what used to be in the past. But God never takes us backward; God always moves us forward. And while we may say we want something new and different in our lives, we are scared to death of change. We only want change if we can control it; if we can regulate the process of what is going to happen and how. But we can't, so it becomes easier to wish for the life we once knew.

But in this season, I want to encourage you to stand in the unknown and not decide you need to go back to Egypt. We can be so afraid that we would rather go back to the slavery we know than the freedom we can't control.

The only time we have a need to control things is when we are overwhelmed by fear. But why are you afraid of God? Who taught you that God is to be feared, that God may not come through for you? Or perhaps you have been conditioned to believe that it is God's will for you to suffer. Nothing could be further from the truth. God is on a mission to set the captives free. But you can't embrace freedom if you have already decided you don't want to be.

Today's Affirmation:

"I am willing to leave the old me behind and embrace my future."

Today's Action:

Write a letter to the past or the old you that you are now committed to leaving behind. This should include old beliefs, old ways of thinking, and old patterns that you are aware of.

Day 4

Soul Surrender

Surrender Your Timeline

"To everything there is a season, a time for everything, and a season for every activity under the heavens."
Ecclesiastes 3:1 (NIV)

"He may not come when you want him, but He is always on time"; at least, that's what the church folks say about God. But "Where are you, God" is what I'm sure you've said more than a few times in your life. And during this surrender, it is critical that you be willing to surrender your timeline, your master plan, and your agenda.

"I should be further along by now," so many people have said, but should you? If there is no place that you can be that God is not, then how in the world can you be out of place? What if I told you there was no such thing as catching up in life? What if every stop and detour on the journey is necessary for your becoming and for your life assignment?

So while you have some things that you need God to do for you, I want to invite you to get in the posture of Divine waiting. This kind of waiting doesn't keep you looking at your life clock. It takes you off the judgment wheel and helps you settle down right where you are.

And while God may have given you a powerful vision that doesn't match your current condition, that doesn't mean that now is the time for that to be your reality. There is such a thing as preparation. There is a thing called Divine timing, where God lines everything up to intersect with you. But in the meantime, we wait, knowing that when the season is right, God will do exactly what was said.

Today's Affirmation:
"I am right where I am supposed to be"

Today's Action:

I invite you to do a mindfulness meditation that allows you to focus on where you are now. Resist the temptation to live into the future. Release your impatience and tell your soul to wait.

Day 5
Soul Surrender

Surrender All Soul Agreements

"And he said to Jacob, quick let me have some of that red stew! I'm famished"; and Jacob replied first sell me your birthright. Look I am about to die, Esau said, what good is a birthright to me?"
Genesis 25: 30-32 (NIV)

Contracts are legally binding agreements that declare what one person will do and what another person will do. We understand what it means to have a contract on a house, contracts with banks for loans, as well as what it means to be a contractor for an employer. But did you know that you also have spiritual contracts that bind you to certain beliefs and behaviors?

And many of these contracts were established by the wounded child within you, who had certain experiences and decided that "this" was what you needed to do and agree to ultimately get love. It all comes down to love.

And as an adult, you now have all kinds of soul agreements in place that keep you quiet, closed off, keep you unhappy, invisible, and telling yourself you will never be good enough. But today is the day you agree to surrender every contract that has made you a hostage to your life.

Understand that you were never in a position to make these agreements in the first place, and according to your Heavenly Father, they are now null and void. A revised contract is now in place that will give you the freedom to be you. You can now spread your wings without apology. All contracts based on fear have been canceled, and your contract to be a whole, healthy soul is in full effect.

Today's Affirmation:

"My contract is with God and what He promised me."

Today's Action:

What agreements did your wounded self make with life? What agreements did you make about love? What contracts did you make with your voice, body, and greatness? What contracts need to be canceled?

Day 6

Soul Surrender

Surrender Your Need to Know The Way

"But he knows the way that I take; when he has tested me, I will come forth as gold."
Job 23:10 (NIV)

You've entered new territory now; you've never been this way before, and that part of you that needs to know all of the details is going crazy. But as one of my professors told me early on in ministry, "following Jesus means giving up your need to know." You have to want God more than you want the answers. And why exactly do you need the answer if God is the one who is in the driver's seat of your life? If the God of the universe is taking you for the ride of a lifetime, why do you need to have all of the directions?

This part of the journey requires you simply sit back and buckle up. Just like a child who trusts his parents to "get him there," you have to ride along with God in the same way. The route may look different; the way may look different than how it looked yesterday but know that you will end up exactly where God promised you would be.

We can be so frantic about where we are going and how we will get there that we can miss the amazing scenery along the way. I admit I love to drive, partly because I like being in control of how fast we go and how we come around those corners on a windy road. But when I sit in that passenger seat and actually relax, I get to gaze at the beautiful trees. I get to see the sights that I would no doubt miss if I was focused on driving an unfamiliar road.

And maybe that's God's point; to get us to enjoy the journey and not be so obsessed about the destination. There is no doubt that life can be a wild ride, but your safety and security is not in knowing the road map but who is in charge of the wheel. So rest yourself. Surrender your need to know the when and how, and just know that you will get there.

Today's Affirmation:

"God knows the way I must take, and I trust Him to get me there."

Today's Action:

Take a look at your life and survey what you have been missing while being overly focused on your process. Look more closely at your relationships and environment and make a list of what you haven't paid much attention to that is a beautiful blessing.

Day 7

Soul Surrender

Surrender Your Anger

"In your anger, do not sin; do not let the sun go down while you are still angry."
Ephesians 4:26 (NIV)

I know you've been taught that good Christian girls don't get angry. We don't cuss, fuss, or throw fits, and for the most part, that is correct. But let me tell you what we do instead. We withhold, go silent, avoid, and eventually implode. There may not be a radical outward display, but make no mistake about it; there is anger and lots of it.

And what exactly are we angry about, you might ask. There are times that we are angry at other people, but in most cases, we are angry at ourselves. There is a place deep down within us that always believes we should have known better, we should have left sooner, or we should have said something. At the end of the day in our world, we believe we are to blame for whatever is happening in our lives.

It is the curse of the woman who sees herself responsible for the whole world. Of course, we would never say that; a statement like that would be ludicrous. But that's exactly how we live. And we are quite angry about it. And anger must have somewhere to go. Anger that does not express itself outwardly is a time bomb inwardly. So the sadness, the depression, the zoning out, and checking out is really deep-rooted anger in disguise.

And as you take this journey back to the essence of yourself, you have to let it go. But how do you surrender what you won't even acknowledge is there. So admitting it has to be the starting place. Realizing that you are a human with real feelings is a beginning. And understanding that it is NOT a sin to be angry; the sin is letting the anger make a home inside you. Because anything that alters the truth of who you are is a sin to God.

And you are not stupid, foolish, or dumb because you let someone mishandle your heart. All of us have moments where we want to believe for the best. And no one is right about everything and everyone all the time. And wisdom does not come from getting it right, but from the times we learn from getting it wrong.

Today's Affirmation:
"I am honest enough to say I am hurt, and I am angry."

Today's Action:

What are you really angry about? Set a 10-minute timer and give yourself permission to literally brain dump on a blank sheet of paper about every offense, every injustice, and circumstance you are holding anger about.

Day 8

Soul Surrender

Surrender the Fight

"For though we live in the world, we do not wage war as the world does."

2 Corinthians 10:3 (NIV)

You were taught to fight, to not give up. Because to stop fighting is to lose, and the last thing you are is a loser. Right??

But a surrendered woman fights differently. She knows her strength is not in her effort but in her quiet movements. You must remember that the weapons we use for warfare are not carnal but spiritual and mighty for the pulling down of strongholds. Your best weapon is not in how hard you hit or how loud you speak, but the center of your power is knowing who God is, which also reminds you who you are.

No one can convince you of anything different when you know what you know. You no longer spend time and energy trying to prove yourself. A woman who has been approved by God has nothing she needs to prove. She has no need to be "right" because who you are won't change, even if you are wrong.

So surrender the invitation to get into every fight. A prizefighter strategically chooses her fight because she is wise enough to know that every battle isn't worth fighting. You must decide to use your energy wisely because a Queen's number one concern is elevating her kingdom. At the end of the day, a woman is not here to tear down but to build up.

Today's Affirmation:

"I don't focus on small battles because I have already won the war."

Today's Action:

Identify the fights you are in and how much it costs you to keep fighting energy-wasting battles. What are you really trying to convince your opponent of? What does winning even look like if you keep fighting the way you have been? Be willing to give it up.

Day 9

Soul Surrender

Surrender your Brokenness

"Heal me, oh God, and I will be healed; save me, and I shall be saved."
Jeremiah 17:14 (NIV)

You can spend your entire life making sure no one sees any cracks in your armor. In this culture, we go out of our way trying to make it look like we have never been bruised, that we can take a licking and keep on ticking.

But understand this, pain unattended doesn't stop being pain. Broken glass that stays on the floor is still dangerous, even if we sweep it under the couch. And I have learned that either we are fixated on the parts of us that are broken, or we are totally ignoring it. But today, you are invited to give it over, to surrender those parts of you that remind you of who hurt you and how. Stop making the details of your pain a meditation that keeps you in a state of acute distress. You can't feel good if you are constantly thinking about when you felt bad.

God is able to give you peace, but you have to be willing to let go. You can't receive joy if your hands are full of broken pieces. You have to make room for joy. Make room for peace. You have to give God what you think is broken if you want it to be made whole again.

Brokenness happens to all of us; no one goes through life without being wounded. But you do have a choice to heal, or you can keep picking the scab and re-injuring yourself over and over again. Your original injury was but a moment in time, and you get to decide if you are going to allow the pain to be with you for a lifetime.

Today's Affirmation:
"I am ready to show God my wounds."

Today's Action:

In your journal, complete this surrender exercise by making a list of the wounds of disappointment, hurt, betrayals, humiliations, and things you are ashamed of ... Each sentence should start with, "I Surrender...." Then be specific about things you know you need to surrender to God, who is able to make things right within. Ex. *"I surrender my embarrassment that I never finished my degree when I know I could have."*

Day 10

Soul Surrender

Surrender your Need to Fix It

"Physician, heal yourself."
Luke 4:23 (NIV)

"If it ain't broke, don't fix it" is what we have always heard, but I say if it is broke, that doesn't mean you have to fix it. I say that to every person who has made it their personal mission in life to fix what they didn't break and repair what they didn't destroy. There is a difference between nurturing the wounded and making yourself a rehab center for every broken person you meet. So today, I invite you to surrender your need to fix it all and get comfortable with people, places, and things in your life being broken and in disarray.

It is human nature to want to help when you see someone in need, so helping in itself is not the problem. When we care more for others than they care for themselves, we get into trouble. And if you have a pattern of always showing up like rescue rangers, it is easy to develop a need to be needed instead of adopting the healthy stance of supporting a person while they do the work of healing.

Why do we want more for people than we want for ourselves? The good girl answer is always about "wanting the best" for others or "seeing their potential,"; but the raw truth is that it is easier to tend to the wounds of others than it is to heal our own. We can see other people in their full potential, but we constantly put ourselves down. We have grace for everyone but no grace for ourselves. You only keep yourself in the dark when you are afraid of your light.

But today, we surrender wanting to work on everyone else and put the spotlight on you. What if you believed in yourself at the level you believe in others? What if you dropped everything at 3 in the morning to help you, to pray for you, to make moves for you, just like you have done for everyone you say you love. It's time out for spending all of your energy taking care of others. This time, your assignment is to fix you.

Today's Affirmation:

"What I have done for others, I now do for myself."

Today's Action:

Make a list of what you helped other people do that you really needed to do for you?

Day 11

Soul Surrender

Surrender your Understanding

"Trust in the Lord with all thine heart and lean not unto your own understanding."
Proverbs 3:5 (NIV)

I love thinking women. I am a thinking woman. But one thing that gets me in trouble is my need to constantly analyze and understand. But one of my mentors once told me that if I am going to be a true disciple of Christ, I have to give up my need to know and understand.

Who can understand the mind of God? Why do bad things happen to good people? Why do certain things seem to happen over and over to certain people? Are we being punished when bad things happen? And are we being blessed because we've been so good? Does God hold a grudge when we mess up? Or can we really earn favor?

God's ways are not like our ways, and His thoughts are higher than our thoughts. And we waste so much time trying to understand why instead of investing our energy in learning how to be right where we are. It really doesn't matter why you are in the situation you are in, but what matters is what you should learn from it. God's lessons are bathed with love, not with guilt and shame. But when we are fixated on why certain things are happening to us or why the people in our lives do what they do, we will surely miss what God wants to reveal to us.

Today's Affirmation:

"I am willing to surrender my why questions, so I can see you."

Today's Action:

Do a yoga practice that challenges you to hold a position or a train of thought while resisting the urge to overthink. In your prayer time, let God know what questions you are now willing to surrender.

Day 12

Soul Surrender

Surrender the Spirit of Lack

"Now unto him who is able to do exceedingly more than you could ever ask, think, or imagine according to the power that is within you."
Ephesians 3:20 (NIV)

Save some for somebody else"; "don't take it all" is what we have always been told. So from childhood, most of us have learned that there just isn't enough to go around, so don't be greedy. But if we are the children of the one who holds the hold earth in His hands, or owns the cattle on a thousand hills, then how could there ever be not enough for us?

The spirit of lack shows up in so many places in our lives, even beyond money. As teenagers, we are programmed to look for "the one" as if there could never be anyone else. Which sets us up to be desperate when that first love doesn't work out. Every woman remembers being that girl who literally cried her eyes out because the love we thought would be forever lasted only three months. So we either tell ourselves, "I will never love again," or go on a mission to find love before time runs out. We have been programmed to hurry up and "get ours" before it's all gone. Go get that money, go get the relationship, go get the perfect house, get the job, and that Instagram life.

But the funny thing is when we "get it," any part of it, we then feel guilty like we stole something from somebody else. We don't just think there isn't enough of the material things, but we unconsciously believe that we can't be "too happy," so anytime life gets "too good," we somehow bring ourselves back to ground zero. But now is the time to surrender the idea of lack. It's time for you to stop scurrying for scraps of bread when God offers you a whole loaf. The kind of bread that promises you will never be hungry again. So feast on your life and get ready for all the love and joy you can stand. There is more than enough.

Today's Affirmation:
"There is more than enough for me."

Today's Action:

Make a list of where you have placed limits on yourself because you have been programmed to believe there is not enough. Where are you acting like there isn't enough money, love, joy? Think about when you brought yourself down because life was getting too good.

Day 13

Soul Surrender

Surrender your Expectations

"And this hope does not put us to shame, because God has poured out his love to fill our hearts."
Romans 5:5 (NIV)

If I had a dollar for every time a woman told me they decided to be with someone because they had potential, I'd be a billionaire by now. You can believe in potential, but actual relationships are with people. And we must be willing to see people for who they are and not for who we want them to be.

When we are wounded, we make choices based on our needs and who we believe will be the missing piece. But nothing outside of you can heal the pain within you. And when we expect anyone or anything to be our everything, we are sure to end up disappointed. Because you don't get what you expect in this life, you get what you require. And the truth is most of us require nothing but expect everything.

You can't expect a broken vessel to provide at full capacity. And all too often, we expect someone else to do what God has called us to do for ourselves. But now is the season to surrender what you expect of others and put your expectation in God, who never disappoints. So much of your sadness has been about what you want someone else to be for you. But they can never be what God can and will. So let whoever you've been holding hostage off the hook. They were never meant to be everything you needed them to be.

Today's Affirmation:

"I place my hope in God who has everything I need."

Today's Action:

Where have you been deeply disappointed because someone or something didn't meet your expectations? Is what you are expecting really realistic based on that person's capacity, or have you been looking at potential? In your prayer time, surrender your need to God.

Day 14

Soul Surrender

Surrender the Fantasy

"In this world, you will have trouble. But take heart, I have overcome the world."
John 16:33 (NIV)

Isn't it supposed to be easier than this? When I watched my life on the screen of my mind, it wasn't designed to be this hard. I thought I was going to wake up happy, love my house, like my job, and have endless adventures every weekend. That's how it plays out on the Hallmark channel when a woman goes about the business of finding herself in the world.

The problem is your life is not on the silver screen. The script you live out didn't come from Hallmark. All too often, you are feeling like an episode of "Iyanla, Fix My Life." Nothing is going as planned. Your relationships are complicated at best. And you seem to be having a hard time saying how you really feel. You keep thinking that you will wake up one day to the rescue squad beating on your door, there to save you. But you've been waiting for years, and no one has shown up yet.

I hate to break it to you, but no one is coming. No one is coming to save you from your life. This is your life, and if you don't like it, it's up to you to change it. As little girls, we were taught to believe in make-believe. Every Disney movie had you convinced that a handsome prince was going to show up and whisk you away. You've been waiting on a gorgeous fairy godmother to come and bestow magical powers on you. But I've come to let you know that you already have all the magic you need. Who needs a fantasy when you have the power to create a powerful reality.

So surrender the fantasy; it only keeps you dreaming of a day that will never come. When you wake up to yourself and who you already are, you will stop waiting for someone or something to save you. But instead, you will create a life that won't make you want to fall into a deep sleep. You will unlock your own magic wand and realize that your every wish is in your own hands.

Today's Affirmation:
"The magic is already within me."

Today's Action:

Think about what you have been waiting for someone else to show up in your life and "save" you from? Spend some time in prayer and meditation and let God reveal to you what you have the power to do for yourself.

Day 15

Soul Surrender

Surrender your Goals

"I am the vine; you are the branches. If you remain in me and I in you, you will bear much fruit; apart from me you can do nothing."
John 15:5 (NIV)

There is nothing wrong with having goals; we are conditioned in western culture to constantly set goals and achieve them. But what happens when your goals don't line up with God's goals? Are you willing to drop your plans for what God has in mind, or do you keep barreling on full speed ahead, hoping God's grace will just cover you?

We must be willing to consider why we can be so fixated on things being our way. Is it really about what we are trying to achieve, or is it the ego that refuses to have it any other way? Because if life is about living out your purpose, isn't it more important to be aligned with God's purpose than your plans? The truth is goals can easily become an idol, something we worship and put above everything else. Just think about yourself or other people you know who just had to be married, had to have a baby, a certain job, or a certain address. We unconsciously treat all of these things like goals rather than part of the journey called life. And whenever we don't get them, in the time frame we wanted them, we tend to do whatever we have to do to get it. Even if that means ignoring and defying God.

But in this season, you must be willing to give your goals to God. It is not God's job to follow your lead; we are following Him. We don't tell God how to bless us; our obedience is how we are to bless Him. And wherever God is, you definitely want to be there. In his presence is the fullness of joy. So it may not be what you planned, but trust that God's way is exactly what you need.

Today's Affirmation:

"I let go of my plans and embrace God's purpose."

Today's Action:

Make an honest list of areas of your life that you have goals that you have you moving full speed ahead no matter what God is showing you. When have you told yourself that your plans are God's plans, even though things are not lining up? What are you really afraid of if you were to surrender your goals?

Day 16

Soul Surrender

Surrender the Weight

"Therefore, since we are surrounded by such a great cloud of witnesses, let us throw off everything that hinders and the sin that so easily entangles. And let us run with perseverance the race marked out for us."

Hebrews 12:1 (NIV)

"Before it was a weight on your body, it was a weight on your mind." That quote is so significant when you understand that your body, mind, and spirit are connected. The thoughts you think and the wounds your soul has endured have a way of showing up on your body. I rarely meet a woman who is deeply distressed in her spirit, who isn't also vexed in her mind, and whose body hasn't also been affected by holding the trauma.

That pain you feel in your neck and shoulders is related to the weight of the world that you have been carrying for years. The fibroids that just won't go away are connected to the unresolved emotions and issues in our relationships that we have stored deep inside. A quote says, "If you don't cry above, you will cry below." And for too many women, our womb is literally crying a thousand tears. We are hurting from the very center of our soul, making it hard for us to create anything. We have been robbed of what real passion and power are.

Remember, pain must have somewhere to go, and if you don't give it an exit, it will find its way to your hips, thighs, and backside. Our bodies are tired, literally exhausted. We either sleep too much or aren't sleeping at all. Our knees are strained, trying to hold it all together. And while we have tried every diet in the book to get the extra weight off, what we need to release first is not the physical; but the mental and the spiritual. We have to stop loading ourselves down with problems that are too big to solve and people too big to carry. I promise, when you let them go, when you say this is too much for me, the weight will be released too.

Today's Affirmation:

"I surrender the heaviness that I carry in my heart and on my body."

Today's Action:

Today notice how you feel when you are stressed and how it is connected to what you decide to eat. Write a goodbye letter to the excess weight that you have been carrying. It may have shown up to protect you, but the surrendered you no longer needs to carry anything that doesn't belong to you.

Day 17

Soul Surrender

Surrender Your Need to Be Liked

"Then Saul said to Samuel, "I have sinned. I violated the LORD's command and your instructions. I was afraid of the men and so I gave in to them."
1 Samuel 15:24 (NIV)

"I wonder will they like me" is a thought I would think throughout much of my childhood, especially being a military brat moving between states and countries growing up. It is natural and normal for children to want to fit in, but as we move into adulthood, this can become problematic when God calls you to stand out. You are different. You are a peculiar woman, part of a royal priesthood, and you will not be able to do what everyone else is doing. So it is essential in this surrender season that you give up your need to be liked.

And when you really think about it, "like" is such a fickle word. What we like today, we can't stand tomorrow. What we like is forever changing. We like strawberry ice cream. We like tv shows and certain cars. It's a preference, but over time preferences change. And the same is true when we make it our business to get other people to like us. Like is just an undercover way to receive validation. When people like us, we believe that we matter and are ok in the world. But when you build your value on "likes," what happens when people decide they don't like you anymore? Your self-esteem takes a deep dive, and you feel devalued. And it also puts you in a position to compromise who you are to get it back. This is exactly what happened to Saul, who was appointed by God to be King over Israel. He was great in size and stature but saw himself very small. And when God gave him very specific instructions about how to handle Israel's enemies, Saul decided to get the approval of people rather than obey God. And because of that one decision, Saul lost his throne.

This is exactly why your validation must come from God. When God has approved you, what higher stamp of approval do you need? When God has affirmed you, something unlocks within you that lets you know you are enough just the way you are. You are not trying to get anything from people because God has given you what you need to give yourself.

You must be willing to like yourself. Liking yourself ensures that you can't be bought, and you won't be deceived because of what you want to hear. You will know the truth about you and what you stand for and be unapologetic about it. So stop jumping through hoops, beautiful one, trying to get them to like you. Stop laughing at jokes that aren't funny and going places you don't even want to be. Come out from the crowd in your attempt to be "one of them." You are not them; be uniquely you. And what good is a temporary like when you are eternally loved?? Surrender the likes, and embrace God's love.

Today's Affirmation:
"God accepts me, likes me, and loves me."

Today's Action:

Think about the many ways you have compromised yourself to get someone or a group of people to like you. What did you really think their approval of you would mean in your life? Reflect on how God's approval is so much greater than anyone else's. Write a list of 10 things that you really like about yourself and read it aloud to yourself.

Day 18

Soul Surrender

I Surrender Those Who Have Wounded Me

"Do not take revenge, my dear friends, but leave room for God's wrath; for it is written, "Vengeance is mine, I will repay says the Lord." Romans 12:19 (NIV)

Hurting people hurt others. That's not just an idea but a fact. People can't give you what they don't have; they can only give you what they have. And sadly, most of the people in this world have nothing but broken glass. So whether they mean to or not, when you interact with them, it is highly probable that you will at some point get cut. Wounds that were never tended to don't just go away, but they continue to bleed. Over time, they will become infected far beyond where the injury first occurred.

And while it is a fact that people have been hurt in their lives, that still doesn't excuse the wound. We can be so quick to psycho-analyze people and why they do what they do that we begin to excuse the wounds that have been inflicted on us. And don't add Christian theology to the mix because we will tell ourselves that "we just have to forgive." And I have heard people say that without having even one conversation. And my response to those people is that you can't forgive what you refuse to acknowledge. We have to understand that forgiveness is a process, and if we don't move through the proper steps, we will not really be released.

I say "you won't be released" because forgiveness is more about you than it is about who wounded you. We have to free ourselves from replaying the incident or the memory of our pain in our heads repeatedly. We have to free ourselves from wanting the other person to pay. We have to release the anger and the rage that is wreaking havoc on the inside. But to do that, we must name the pain and the person who inflicted it. We may not be responsible for who hurt us, but we are responsible for healing it. So surrender whoever you have been holding hostage for your sake. Now is the time to make peace with you.

Today's Affirmation:

"**You chose to hurt me, but I choose to heal me.**"

Today's Action:

Make a list of the people you know you need to forgive, people that make you agitated even when you hear their name or see them. Whether it is someone you see once a year or every day, name them, name the offense, and release them to God so you can be free.

Day 19

Soul Surrender

I Surrender My Mother & Father

"When my father and my mother forsake me,
Then the LORD will take care of me."
Psalm 27:10 (NIV)

Since we have already opened up the forgiveness box, we must lean all the way in. This Surrender process is about your healing. It's not just about letting go of what no longer serves you, but it is about healing the root cause of those decisions in the first place. And while we love our parents, even if they were unhealthy, it is now time to heal our relationship with them. Whether they are living or have transitioned to the next life, we surrender what was and what we wish they would have been, not for them, but for you. This is for the healing you need in your soul.

Regardless of the soul wound we carry, every wound can be traced back to a parent. If it is not connected to what they did, it comes back to what they didn't do. The fear that creeps into the lining of our hearts is more about what was missing and not what we had. So we can spend a lifetime either looking for a way to fill the gap or controlling everything trying to make sure what hurt us "never happens again." But what exactly happened in our relationship with mommy or daddy? We confuse "honoring your mother and father" with ignoring and avoiding the truth. We have been taught that people can't handle the truth. But it is not the truth that hurts but living a lie.

When we surrender our relationship with our mother or father to God, what we are really doing is acknowledging they did the best they could do with what they had. And given that so many soul wounds run through generations, we must recognize that they are wounded people just like us. So let go of what you wish your childhood would have been like, and accept that what the devil meant for evil, God is turning around for your good. But to step into the power of your experiences, you have to stop wishing the past could have been different. So surrender mom with her criticism or inability to be available the way you needed her. Let dad off the hook because he was a father who had not yet learned what it meant to be a man. And stop torturing yourself, thinking God was punishing you. It was never about punishment but your divine preparation.

Today's Affirmation:
"Everything I have gone through has only prepared me for now."

Today's Action:

Repeat yesterday's life work but focus specifically on your mom and dad's specific memories or the lack of memories you need to give to God. Tell God you are tired and are ready to give them over.

Day 20

Soul Surrender

I Surrender My Beliefs

"Immediately, the boy's father exclaimed, I do believe, but help my unbelief."
Mark 9:14 (NIV)

Every time I think I understand what's going on, God presents me with a circumstance that lets me know I don't. And don't ask me why I am constantly trying to figure out what God is doing and working on anyway. Part of it is control, which by now you realize is an illusion. But the other part of needing to understand and figure it all out is a way of locking in my beliefs. A part of us needs to know how God works and what we can expect living in this world.

But God's ways are not our ways. His thoughts are certainly not my thoughts. That's why there are often no words or answers for life's difficult situations. No one really knows why bad things happen to good people. And when you're dealing with God, who even knows what bad is anymore? What we do know is the stuff that doesn't feel good. We know what pain is. We know what it feels like when it literally feels like your heart is outside of our chest.

During those times, I urge you to not go into deep psychoanalysis. That is not the time to get into a theological debate about the Bible and what certain scriptures mean. In these moments, all we have to cling to is who God says He is. Even if you don't understand it or can't explain it to others, can you accept that He is God? And while you may not know what to believe about all the details of the story of your life, are you willing to still believe you know how the story ends.

This is a hard one, especially in a culture where you are encouraged to know what you believe at all times about everything. But there will be times when life leaves you speechless. Surrender and lean into that when you don't know what to believe. Don't fight it or force it. Simply believe what you can, and let God help you with the rest.

Today's Affirmation:
"I believe that God is still God, and that is enough."

Today's Action:

What are you wrestling with God and yourself about? What situation and circumstances have you questioning what you thought was the truth? Be emotionally honest with yourself and write your thoughts in a journal as a conversation with God. And know that God can handle the questions that others can't.

Day 21

Soul Surrender

I Surrender My Imperfections

"I will praise you because I am fearfully and wonderfully made. Your works are wonderful and I know that full well."
Psalm 139:14 (NIV)

"Who told you that?" is a question I often ask my clients when they describe themselves with negative traits. Most of us are merely repeating someone else's perception of us; we have heard it so many times that even though we doubted it at first, we have adopted it as our own truth over time. Things like, "I'm shy,"; "I don't speak well," or "I'm a disorganized person"; sometimes you have to stop the tape and ask yourself, "Is this really true?.." And even if it is, why do we always seem to shine a spotlight on our flaws while we are quick to overlook and dismiss our strengths?

The bottom line is we have decided we are not enough. We are flawed and somehow disqualified from fully participating in the world. If you don't believe me, then check out the excuses you make to yourself whenever a new opportunity presents itself. What are the reasons you justify staying where you are? And I bet that 9 times out of 10, we don't think we are enough for the task.

But I dare you to stop focusing on the parts of you that aren't perfect. Stop creating a standard that you or nobody else will ever meet. Sadly many of us were doubted and told we weren't good enough as children and have only continued this hurtful thinking into adulthood. Those negative voices passed the baton years ago, and we didn't know any better than to pick it up.

Some people are less gifted and less talented, leaping from chandeliers and taking their shot at life. We forget that leaping is the joy we seek in this life, not being perfect and never making mistakes. Just ask any inventor or successful entrepreneur. They had to be ok with not being ok while still moving forward. And perfection was never God's instruction, but rather faithfulness is what God wants. So let go and leap in. Trust that who you are right now is enough for where God wants you to go. Your soul will thank you later.

Today's Affirmation:
"I am the perfect person to do what God has called me to do."

Today's Action:

What is the negative chatter that continues to show up in your head that keeps you from moving forward? Ask yourself if it's really true? Who actually told you this? And what does it really have to do with what you have been assigned to do at this moment?

Day 22

Soul Surrender

I Surrender to Love

I pray that out of his glorious riches he may strengthen you with power through his Spirit in your inner being, 17 so that Christ may dwell in your hearts through faith. And I pray that you, being rooted and established in love, 18 may have power, together with all the Lord's holy people, to grasp how wide and long and high and deep is the love of Christ,
Ephesians 3:16-18 (NIV)

While it is important to let go of everything that has hurt you and forgive, we must also be intentional about filling up the empty space. And there is nothing better than love to fill you. Love is not what other people do for you, but what you decide to do for yourself. So much of the hurt we have endured has to do with the fact that we have not filled ourselves up; we expected other people to do it. And when that didn't happen, we either kept looking or settled on being empty.

But empty isn't an option for the fully surrendered woman. You must be filled with the beauty of love if you are going to be led by God's will and not your appetite. And without love, you are hungry. Hunger makes you vulnerable; it makes you not see what's right in front of you.

So today, we surrender to love, which means we lean into it. We believe we are loveable and loved. We surrender to the kind of love that welcomes good things in our lives. The opposite of love is not hate but fear. And as we let go of fear, we do so knowing that we are safe and covered by God's love. So even when life presents circumstances that we can't and don't understand, we surrender to love. When your whole world changes and you realize you were never in control, you lean into love.

So bathe yourself in God's love. Drink from the cup of God's love, with the promise that your soul will never be thirsty again. If we can't resist loving a newborn baby, then know that nothing can resist God's love for you. So close your eyes; open your heart, and get ready to experience a love you have never known. As one writer beautifully wrote, "I found God in myself, and I loved her fiercely."

Today's Affirmation:
"I am loved more than I could ever know."

Today's Action:

Close your eyes and literally feel yourself being covered by God's love for you. Do this several times a day, and soak it in. Do one thing today that demonstrates the love you have for yourself.

Day 23

Soul Surrender

I Surrender to Peace

"Peace I leave with you; my peace I give you. I do not give to you as the world gives. Do not let your hearts be troubled, and do not be afraid."

John 14:27 (NIV)

You have prayed for peace in your life more times than you can count, but do you really know what to do when you get it? Some of you have been at war for so long that you don't know what to do when there is nothing and no one to fight. And if by chance you have been programmed to be the rebel or to be "ready," we end up forfeiting our peace because all we know is the fight.

It may sound crazy to think that anyone would reject peace, but our refusal to rest in this gift is really a confession about how we don't trust that it will last. So instead of waiting for the carpet to be ripped from under you, you throw the carpet out the window yourself. So what comes first, the chicken or the egg, the chaos or our need to create it??

But peace is not an aromatherapy candle or a nice hot bubble bath. Peace comes from within. And no one takes it away. We simply decide to give it up. But today, you make a different choice. To receive God's peace and live in peace. Regardless of the chaos going on around you, crazy can't come in unless you open the door. And just because you've been in the habit of entertaining crazy and foolishness in the past doesn't mean you can't make a different choice in this moment for your future.

God has given you a precious gift, and now is the time for you to surrender your soul to receive it. Let go of the habit of putting yourself through the spin cycle of chaos. Stop acting like fighting is your norm. And let yourself rest in God's peace. This is the place you were always meant to be.

Today's Affirmation:

"I surrender my mind and soul to God's peace and choose not to give it away."

Today's Action:

Think about someone you deeply admire who really knows how to be at peace. Whenever you feel tempted to go into chaos, even if it's just in your mind, think about what that person would do and do it.

Day 24

Soul Surrender

I Surrender to an Abundant Life

"The thief comes to steal, kill and destroy, but I have come that you might have life, and have it more abundantly."
John 10:10 (NIV)

Is there such a thing as life being "too good"? Can a person be "too happy"? Well, most of us say we want to be happy; we say we want God to bless us, but the question is will you allow yourself to be blessed? Most of us have an interesting relationship with pain and suffering; we have become used to being disappointed. We are used to being hurt. And some of us unconsciously feel that we have been destined to suffer. So much so that when God does bless your life, you don't enjoy it; you simply wait for the other shoe to drop.

"How long is this going to last," is what we begin to say to ourselves. Blocking God's blessings is really denying God's abundance. Most of us have been trained to believe that there isn't enough to go around. Just think about what you were told when you wanted more food, clothes, food, or money growing up. "Money doesn't grow on trees," is what we were told, which really means money must be hard to come by. Our thoughts about money begin to bleed over into how we think about love, joy, and happiness. We start to feel guilty if life gets too good, like we are taking something from somebody else if God chooses to bless us.

But as you surrender what has been holding you back, it is imperative that you also surrender to what God has in store for you. And you don't get to say when it is enough. If God says He will pour out a blessing that you don't even have room to receive, then why do you keep coming to God with a teacup? You are being called to increase your capacity to receive. If you want to be a blessing, you must let God bless you. So surrender to the abundant life that God has planned for you and stop settling for "just enough" and the bare minimum. A child of the King doesn't settle for crumbs, especially when your inheritance is the whole bakery.

Today's Affirmation:

"I open myself to receive everything God has for me."

Today's Action:

Think about a time when life felt so good, so good that you were afraid it wouldn't last, so you either sabotaged it or decided you didn't deserve it. Write a commitment statement to do life differently. "From this day forward, I open myself to receive...."

Day 25

Soul Surrender

I Surrender to the Flow

Whether you turn to the right or to the left, your ears will hear a voice behind you, saying, "This is the way; walk in it."
Isaiah 30:21 (NIV)

There is a way that "seems" right to a woman, but all too often, that "way" leads to pain and disappointment. I had found this out the hard way, as I can't even tell you how many times I thought I knew what was best, when something needed to happen in my life, and all the doors I KICKED open only to wish I had kept them closed. To surrender means to "give up the fight"; to "submit," and to "willfully" give up my power to be under a greater power. And as we come to the 25th day of the Soul Surrender, you must stop going against the grain and get in the flow of the river of your life.

And you do this not because you have to, but the very nature of surrender is you want to. Women have been taught that surrender and submission is a position of weakness, but in reality, it takes more strength to humbly give up your power than it does to forcefully exert it. When we surrender to God, we allow His power to be the guiding force over our lives. And if you really believe that God loves you and has a plan that will bless you and not harm you, then what are you really resisting?

Favor is in the flow. Experiencing God's faithfulness happens in the flow. And the future you've been praying for is right there in your flow. The flow is the place in your life that feels like ease. It is what you naturally know you are supposed to do. It does not always follow logic or what the crowd is saying. But it is that inner GPS that tells you and only you, "this is the way"; "he/she is the one"; or "this is it." It is that place within you that just feels right. So while you have been trained to ignore your feelings, the flow is exactly what you are feeling. So today, step into this holy place that knows, even though you don't know how you know. Stop letting other people tell you the plan when God has already spoken the plan. Trust the way you have never seen, but your soul knows.

Today's Affirmation:
"I flow with God because He knows the blueprint for my future."

Today's Action:

What part of your life is out of sync? Where do you know you are not in a place of flow but forcing things to happen? In your prayer time today, specifically ask God to give you a blueprint specific to you, then flow with it.

Day 26

Soul Surrender

I Surrender to My Growth

"You did not choose me, but I chose you, that you might bear much fruit, fruit that will last."
John 15:16 (NIV)

If you are not growing, you are dying. That may sound like a strong statement, but it is oh so true. Just think about what happens to a plant, a tree, or stagnant water. If those things are not growing and reproducing, then they dry up, start to stink, and die. But unlike the plant world, the way of the human being is not just to grow physically, but to grow mentally, spiritually, and emotionally as well. And that growth doesn't happen by age; it comes only through experience.

So the more experiences you have, the more you grow. That means if you truly want to grow, you have to risk failing at something new. You have to be willing to "not get it right" every time. Every great person in history made multiple attempts to achieve whatever they were trying to accomplish. Just imagine if the Wright brothers had stopped after their first attempt to fly. What if Albert Einstein said forget it after his 50th attempt at the light bulb? What if Madame CJ Walker quit after her product didn't sell? And I can think of countless others who "failed" or didn't get selected when they had a million-dollar idea. They took those difficult experiences, learned what not to do, and decided to do something different.

So stop taking your mistakes or perceived failures as a sign that you were never supposed to try in the first place. Your pain is simply preparing you for a greater purpose. Even the pain we inflict upon ourselves by our own poor choices or disobedience, God is able to work it together for your growth. God is not trying to make you a success; God's goal is to make you more like him, and that is true success.

Today's Affirmation:
"I am committed to grow with God."

Today's Action:

You can't grow if you never take a risk or do anything different. Think about some opportunities that you could have stepped into, but you were too afraid you would fail. Let God know you are ready to grow now; then get ready for God to open the door. Also, think about some areas you think you failed, but now ask yourself what you learned and how did you grow?

Day 27

Soul Surrender

I Surrender My Resistance to Receive Support

"You and these people who come to you will only wear yourselves out. The work is too heavy for you; you cannot handle it alone."
Exodus 18:18 (NIV)

Just because you can do it yourself doesn't mean you need to. There are some things you don't have to do all by yourself. But because you have become accustomed to being left alone and holding the bag, you take on the weight of everything in your life without any assistance. In fact, our culture has glorified stress and strain. We have silent competitions to see who can carry and handle the most. But look around. Carrying everything on your back is taking its toll. We can no longer afford to keep saying, "I got it," because when it comes to the long game of life, we don't.

God does not want you breaking down in your body and spirit 10 yards before the finish line. What good is it to spend a lifetime working and sacrificing but never see the promise? When Moses was leading the people to the Promised Land, he started by trying to do it all himself. He thought everything was on him because God called him to be a leader. But when his father-in-law came to visit and saw the numerous issues that Moses was trying to manage, he immediately told him to put people and systems in place that would hold his arms up. He could see that what Moses was doing wasn't sustainable and the people were going to wear him out if he didn't get some help.

And perhaps you are the same way. Perhaps you have also misunderstood the assignment to lead as a mandate to do it all. You watched your mother and aunts do it all, and you believe that's the way you have to live life too. But today, God is calling you to surrender your resistance to receiving help and support. You need energy for more than the task right in front of you, but you will be depleted if you constantly give away everything you have.

And while people may have let you down in the past, understand that "this" is not "that." The past is over, and this is a new day, so allow yourself a new experience. Break the generational cycle of a lifetime of stress, high blood pressure, and anxiety. Those before you didn't know they could lift up their hands and let it go, but you do. You serve a God who is more than able, and God will send you the help you need. The question is, will you be surrendered enough to receive it.

Today's Affirmation:
"I love myself enough to let myself be supported."

Today's Action:

What area of your life are you overloaded in? Where could you use support to ease your own stress, although you could push yourself to do it all yourself? Where is God nudging you to let go and delegate in your life and/ or business? What is "doing it all" costing you emotionally, spiritually, and physically? Make a decision about at least one area you will let yourself receive support. Share your decision with another person who can keep you accountable.

Day 28

Soul Surrender

I Surrender to My Greatness

"No one lights a lamp and puts it in a place where it will be hidden, or under a bowl. Instead, they put it on its stand so that those who come in may see the light."
Luke 11:33 (NIV)

"Our deepest fear is not that we are inadequate, but our deepest fear is that we are powerful beyond measure. It is our light, not our darkness, that frightens us." This quote by Marianne Williamson is one of my favorites for so many reasons. And on this 28th day of the Soul Surrender, I want to invite you to stop telling yourself that you are afraid to fail when the truth is you have been afraid to succeed.

With all this emphasis in America on being a success and being a BOSS, why would anyone be afraid of success? But when you have spent a lifetime playing small, sitting on the back row, speaking in a whisper, and promoting everyone else's dream other than your own, average can easily become where you think you are supposed to be. And anytime we elevate, stand out, or find ourselves being the "only one," we find a way to "bring ourselves back down to earth." Because who are we to be so great? Who are you to shine so bright?

But surrendering is not about giving up your power, but all about letting God direct that power. And God is preparing to take you to places you never expected you would be. And instead of telling yourself that luck brought you in the room, you must understand that God purposely opened the door and destined for you to have a seat at the table. So it will be up to you to make sure you aren't sitting there acting like it's an accident or apologizing for being there.

You owe it to yourself to take yourself seriously, to know that you were meant for more. You have to know that God has given you amazing power, and you are a chosen vessel, here to do God's will. So your goal is not to try and seek greatness but to realize greatness is already within you. Your assignment is to release that greatness into the world without apology. This is your new surrender.

Today's Affirmation:

"I surrender to my greatness being on full display."

Today's Action:

Make a list of your spiritual and physical gifts and pray a prayer of surrender that allows God to use those gifts. Commit yourself to being seen and shining brightly.

Day 29

Soul Surrender

I Surrender to Making Space in My Life

"Enlarge your house; build an addition. Spread out your home and spare no expense! For you will soon be bursting at the seams. Your descendants will occupy other nations and resettle the ruined cities.
Isaiah 54:2-3 (NIV)

Everyone and everything can't go with you. As much as you love people and want the best for them, understand that when you commit yourself to a life of surrender, you are also giving God permission to decide who and what will go with you on the journey called your life. And just because a person starts with you doesn't mean they will finish. Remember, many are called, but few are chosen. And when God says there must be a separation, a kind of goodbye, then we must be willing to let go.

So as we are nearing the end of our 30 days together, God is saying…. Make room. God requires space in your life, first of all for His presence, and secondly for what He wants to bring to you. You can't receive "this" while you are still holding on to "that." And whenever we refuse to let go, we are really saying we don't believe there will be anything more. And some of us hoard material things and memorabilia as if we will never have another memory again. Why are some of us still holding on to high school or college papers or trinkets? Why are we holding on to pictures of old lovers when that time has long passed? The space you need to make is not just in your hall closet or your garage; the most important space is the one in your mind.

It's time to say goodbye to yesterday if you are really serious about experiencing a "better day." So get ready for some soul cleaning in addition to the spring cleaning that is long overdue. Give God some room to work in your life. Your outer environment is just a reflection of the internal environment. So no more stacks of God knows what stacked up in the corner; no more food that should have been thrown out weeks ago. No more holding on to people who don't know how to treat you; whatever it is, it's time to let it go. God is preparing something fresh and new for your soul. It's time you made yourself ready.

Today's Affirmation:

"I surrender all mental and physical clutter to make room for what God has for me."

Today's Action:

Time to throw some things away. Time to say goodbye to old memories that keep you living in the past. No more holding on to things from another season if you expect God to create a new season. No lingering and overthinking, just let it go. Bye, Felicia... or maybe it's Bye, Fred.

Day 30

Soul Surrender

Surrender to Your Own Becoming

He said, "Can I not do with you, Israel, as this potter does?" declares the LORD. "Like clay in the hand of the potter, so are you in my hand, Israel. Jeremiah 18:6 (NIV)

This life is a journey. It is certainly not a destination; we definitely should have been there already if it was. When I was in my 20's, I thought all the twist and turns of life was because I was messing up. I thought I was doing something wrong.

But as time and life went on, I began to understand that the detours and dead ends in life were all part of it. Getting to "the goal" wasn't really the point, but God's goal was who I was becoming in the process. This is why the journey is always so much more interesting than the feeling we actually get where we think we have to be.

We are all on the potter's wheel, and life is for the molding and shaping of you. God's desire is that you look and function like what He intended. And when we aren't quite there, like the potter, God pushes and reshapes the clay into another form.

Everyone wants to be a vessel, but nobody wants to be shaped. But that's what spiritual surrender is all about. It is understanding that you never know more than the potter. It is humbly submitting to God's design over your own.

The good news is everything the Potter makes is excellent. It is perfect for the purpose for which it was designed. And while we think we know why we are here, honestly, God is the author and publisher of the book of your life. What you know is only part of the story; God knows the whole.

So just like you wouldn't attempt to give somebody directions to where you have never been, perhaps it's time to stop trying to tell God the way your life should go. You have no idea who you really are and what you are here for. And it is only when you surrender to becoming that you are guaranteed to get there.

So on this final day of our surrender journey, I pray this is your new beginning. I pray that this is the day you let God shape and mold your life. Go where He wants you to go and say what He wants you to say. Because ultimately, it's not about anything "out there" but about what you allow God to do with you in here. What you allow in your heart becomes the blueprint for who you will become in your life.

Today's Affirmation:
"I willingly place my life in your hands."

Today's Action:

Instead of looking at the parts of your life and journey that you don't like as if it is a mistake, choose to see things differently and write down the many ways that YOU have evolved because of those things.

Next Steps

You made it through the 30-day surrender! Now what? Your check-the-box nature may have you wondering what's next. First, celebrate your completion. Too often, we don't give ourselves credit for what we complete. We are slow to acknowledge the little things but understand surrendering to God for 30 days straight is no small thing. We are constantly at war with our flesh, and that flesh is always opposed to the Spirit of God that is within you. (Galatians 5:17) So acknowledge and celebrate yourself because what gets rewarded gets repeated.

You have to see this surrender as so much more than a spiritual exercise or daily ritual. These past 30 days have been a time of preparation for what God wants to do in your life. But before you can be used for God's agenda, you have to let go of your own. God needed to strip you of what you wanted and how you felt it needed to be delivered to you so you might be open to other ways. These past 30 days were designed to remind you that you are clay; God is the potter. The Soul Surrender makes you malleable in the hands of God. And while you may have started in resistance, spiritual surrender over time feels like freedom. Surrender removes the self-imposed pressure to "get it right." It is a reminder that in your own self, you don't even know what "right" is. Surrender reminds you that you don't know what you think you know; and that your God knows all.

Spiritual preparation is required because you now understand that you are not your own. You are not just God's beloved but God's vessel. And now that you're empty, ask God to fill you up.

What's next for you? I don't know, but does it really matter? What matters most is not where you are going but who you are going with. More than anything, God wants you. God doesn't just want to use you; God wants to show you how much He loves you. So, may your heart stay in a posture of surrender and availability to God. There is no greater place than where He is.